Velociraptor

Aaron Carr

www.av2books.com

Go to **www.av2books.com**, and enter this book's unique code.

BOOK CODE

F972333

AV² by Weigl brings you media enhanced books that support active learning.

AV² provides enriched content that supplements and complements this book. Weigl's AV² books strive to create inspired learning and engage young minds in a total learning experience.

Your AV² Media Enhanced books come alive with...

Audio
Listen to sections of the book read aloud.

Key Words
Study vocabulary, and complete a matching word activity.

Video
Watch informative video clips.

Quizzes
Test your knowledge.

Embedded Weblinks
Gain additional information for research.

Slide Show
View images and captions, and prepare a presentation.

Try This!
Complete activities and hands-on experiments.

... and much, much more!

Published by AV² by Weigl
350 5th Avenue, 59th Floor New York, NY 10118
Website: www.av2books.com   www.weigl.com

Library of Congress Control Number: 2013937453
ISBN 978-1-62127-243-4 (hardcover)
ISBN 978-1-62127-249-6 (softcover)

Printed in the United States of America in North Mankato, Minnesota
2 3 4 5 6 7 8 9 0 18 17 16 15 14

012014
WEP030114

Project Coordinator: Aaron Carr   Art Director: Terry Paulhus

All illustrations by Jon Hughes, pixel-shack.com; Alamy: 19 inset; Eduard Solà Vázquez: 20.

Velociraptor

In this book,
you will learn

what its
name means

what it
looked like

where it lived

what it ate

and much more!

Meet the Velociraptor.
Its name means
"speedy thief."

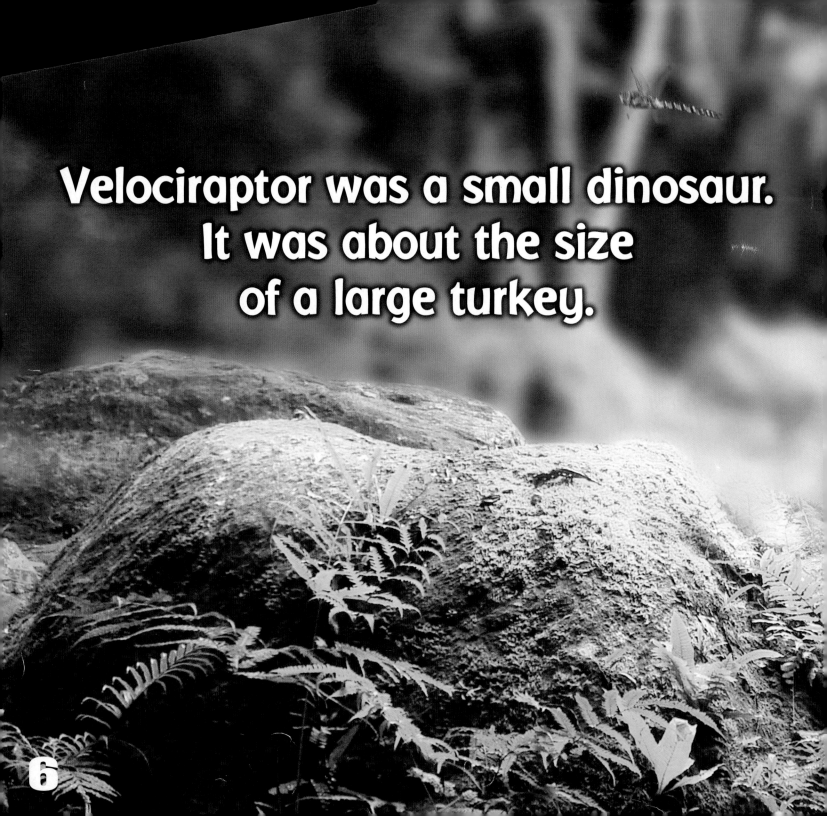

Velociraptor was a small dinosaur. It was about the size of a large turkey.

Velociraptor had a long, sharp claw on each foot.

It used these claws
to catch its food.

Velociraptor was a meat eater.
It hunted small plant-eating
dinosaurs for food.

Velociraptor was one of the smartest dinosaurs that ever lived.

It may have hunted
with other Velociraptors.

Velociraptor ran
on two strong legs.

It may have run
more than 40 miles an hour.

15

Velociraptor lived in places that were hot and dry.

16

It lived in parts of Asia.

Velociraptors died out about 80 million years ago.

People know about Velociraptor because of fossils.

People can go to museums to see fossils and learn more about the Velociraptor.

21

Velociraptor Facts

These pages provide detailed information that expands on the interesting facts found in the book. They are intended to be used by adults as a learning support to help young readers round out their knowledge of each amazing dinosaur or pterosaur featured in the *Discovering Dinosaurs* series.

Pages 4–5

Velociraptor means "speedy thief." The Velociraptor is one of the best-known of all dinosaurs. However, the real Velociraptor was very different from the one people know from movies such as *Jurassic Park*. Unlike the large, scaly raptors seen in movies, the real Velociraptor was much smaller and had feathers. Some scientists believe the Velociraptor may have been entirely covered in feathers, like a bird.

Pages 6–7

Velociraptor was a small dinosaur. The Velociraptor was about 6 feet (1.8 meters) long and 3 feet (1 m) tall. It may have weighed between 15 and 33 pounds (7 and 15 kilograms). Some relatives of the Velociraptor were larger than others. Deinonychus was the largest of these dinosaurs, with a length of 12 feet (3.7 m) and a weight of 150 pounds (68 kg). Most Velociraptors, however, were about the size of a large turkey.

Pages 8–9

Velociraptor had a long, sharp claw on each foot. Each sickle-shaped claw was 3.5 inches (9 centimeters) long. A retractable claw was located on the second toe of each foot. The Velociraptor used its claws to hunt for food and to defend itself from predators. Scientists believe the Velociraptor may have used its tail and one foot for balance while it slashed at its prey with the other foot.

Pages 10–11

Velociraptor was a carnivore, or meat-eater. Scientists believe the Velociraptor preyed on small herbivorous dinosaurs, such as Protoceratops and hadrosaurs. Many scientists believe the Velociraptor hunted in packs to take down larger prey. However, there is no direct evidence to support this theory. Some scientists have suggested that the Velociraptor may have been a scavenger.

KEY WORDS

Research has shown that as much as 65 percent of all written material published in English is made up of 300 words. These 300 words cannot be taught using pictures or learned by sounding them out. They must be recognized by sight. This book contains 48 common sight words to help young readers improve their reading fluency and comprehension. This book also teaches young readers several important content words, such as proper nouns. These words are paired with pictures to aid in learning and improve understanding.

Page	Sight Words First Appearance
4	its, means, name, the
6	a, about, it, large, of, small, was
8	each, had, long, on
9	food, these, to, used
11	for, plant
12	lived, one, that
13	have, may, other, with
14	two
15	an, miles, more, run, than
16	and, in, places, were
17	parts
18	out, years
19	because, know, people
20	can, go, learn, see

Page	Content Words First Appearance
4	thief, Velociraptor (pronounced: veh-loss-ih-RAP-tor)
6	dinosaur, turkey
8	claw, foot
11	meat eater
14	legs
15	hour
17	Asia
19	fossils
20	museums

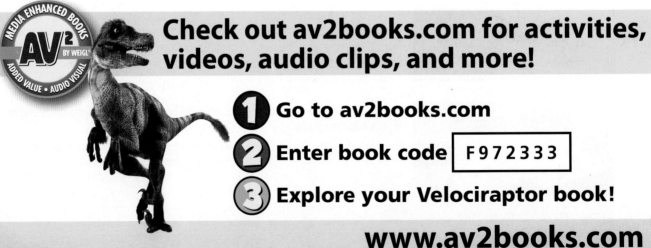